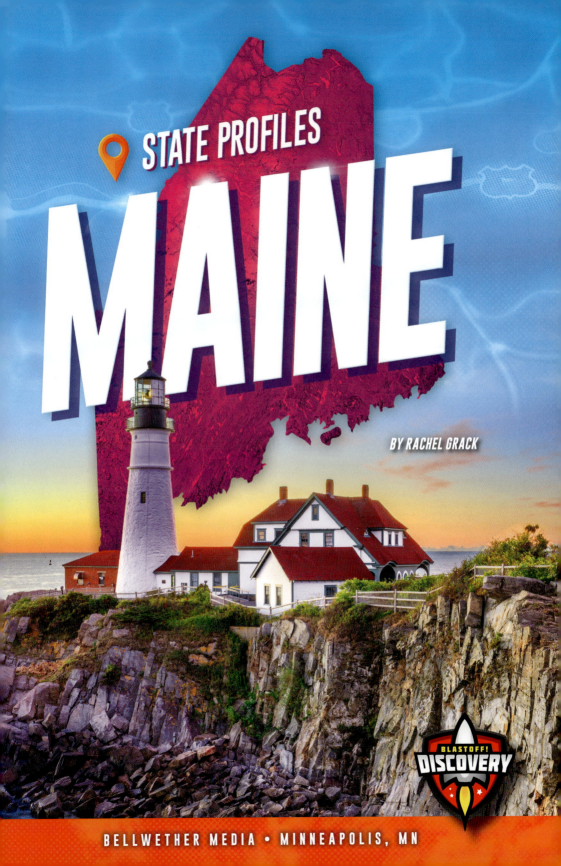

Blastoff! Discovery launches a new mission: reading to learn. Filled with facts and features, each book offers you an exciting new world to explore!

This edition first published in 2022 by Bellwether Media, Inc.

No part of this publication may be reproduced in whole or in part without written permission of the publisher.
For information regarding permission, write to Bellwether Media, Inc., Attention: Permissions Department,
6012 Blue Circle Drive, Minnetonka, MN 55343.

Library of Congress Cataloging-in-Publication Data

Names: Koestler-Grack, Rachel A., 1973- author.
Title: Maine / by Rachel Grack.
Description: Minneapolis, MN : Bellwether Media, Inc., 2022. | Series: Blastoff! Discovery: State profiles | Includes bibliographical references and index. | Audience: Ages 7-13 | Audience: Grades 4-6 | Summary: "Engaging images accompany information about Maine. The combination of high-interest subject matter and narrative text is intended for students in grades 3 through 8"– Provided by publisher.
Identifiers: LCCN 2021019673 (print) | LCCN 2021019674 (ebook) | ISBN 9781644873908 (library binding) | ISBN 9781648341670 (ebook)
Subjects: LCSH: Maine–Juvenile literature.
Classification: LCC F19.3 .K64 2022 (print) | LCC F19.3 (ebook) | DDC 974.1–dc23
LC record available at https://lccn.loc.gov/2021019673
LC ebook record available at https://lccn.loc.gov/2021019674

Text copyright © 2022 by Bellwether Media, Inc. BLASTOFF! DISCOVERY and associated logos are trademarks and/or registered trademarks of Bellwether Media, Inc.

Editor: Betsy Rathburn   Designer: Andrea Schneider

Printed in the United States of America, North Mankato, MN.

TABLE OF CONTENTS

Cadillac Mountain	4
Where Is Maine?	6
Maine's Beginnings	8
Landscape and Climate	10
Wildlife	12
People and Communities	14
Portland	16
Industry	18
Food	20
Sports and Entertainment	22
Festivals and Traditions	24
Maine Timeline	26
Maine Facts	28
Glossary	30
To Learn More	31
Index	32

CADILLAC MOUNTAIN

CADILLAC MOUNTAIN
ACADIA NATIONAL PARK

On a sunny fall morning, a van nears the peak of Cadillac Mountain. A family is visiting the popular Acadia National Park. The parking lot is bustling with hikers heading for the trail to the overlook. The family joins the crowd on the path to the top. Soon, they reach the top of a rocky slope.

OTHER TOP SITES

GULF HAGAS

NUBBLE LIGHTHOUSE

OLD FORT WESTERN

PORTLAND OBSERVATORY

The view from the top is incredible. The sparkling blue waters of the Atlantic Ocean stretch for miles. Tree-covered islands dot the coast. The family can just make out the rooftops of distant houses far below. Welcome to Maine!

WHERE IS MAINE?

Maine is in the northeastern United States. It has an area of 35,380 square miles (91,634 square kilometers). It is the largest state in **New England** and the 39th largest state in the country. Its capital city, Augusta, sits along the Kennebec River in southwestern Maine.

Maine shares its long, straight western border with New Hampshire. Canada is to the northwest, north, and east. The Atlantic Ocean lies to the southeast. Thousands of islands dot the coast, including Mount Desert Island. This is Maine's largest island!

CANADA

CANADA

MAINE

KENNEBEC
RIVER

BANGOR

NEW
HAMPSHIRE

AUGUSTA

MOUNT DESERT
ISLAND

LEWISTON

ATLANTIC
OCEAN

PORTLAND

SMALL CITIES

Only three cities in Maine have more
than 30,000 residents! They are
Portland, Lewiston, and Bangor.

MAINE'S BEGINNINGS

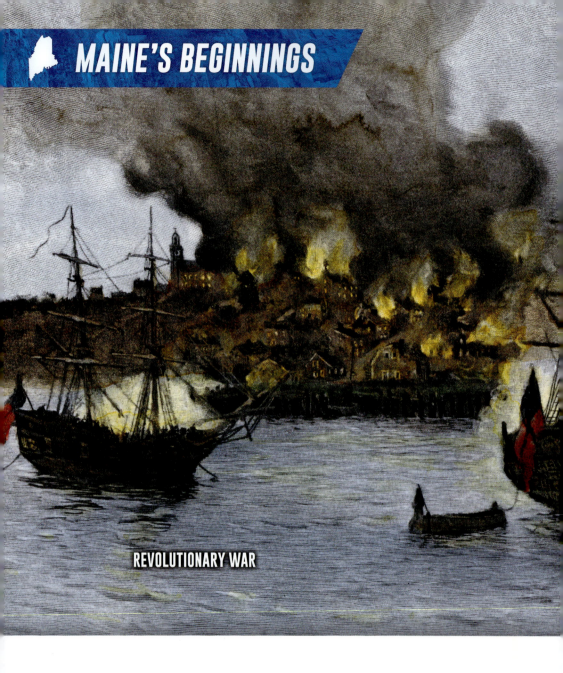

REVOLUTIONARY WAR

People arrived in Maine around 13,000 years ago. The Micmac and Abenaki people were among the first. In time, other Native American tribes formed, including the Penobscot, Passamaquoddy, and Maliseet. They hunted and fished throughout Maine's land and water.

In 1607, English **settlers** established the Popham **Colony** in Maine. The colony failed, but the English built more settlements throughout the 1600s. In the 1770s, people from Maine fought the English in the **Revolutionary War**. After the war, Maine was a part of present-day Massachusetts. The two states separated in 1820, when Maine became the 23rd state.

NATIVE PEOPLES OF MAINE

AROOSTOOK BAND OF MICMAC INDIANS

- Original lands in northern Maine and the Canadian provinces of Quebec, New Brunswick, Nova Scotia, Newfoundland, and Prince Edward Island
- Around 1,490 members today
- Also called L'nu

HOULTON BAND OF MALISEET INDIANS

- Original lands in northern Maine and the Canadian provinces of Quebec and New Brunswick
- Around 1,700 members today
- Also called Wolastoqiyik

PENOBSCOT

- Original lands covered northeastern and eastern Maine
- Around 2,400 members today

PASSAMAQUODDY

- Original lands included northeastern Maine and parts of Canada
- Around 3,600 members today

LANDSCAPE AND CLIMATE

The Appalachian Mountains cover much of northwestern Maine. The range tapers off at Mount Katahdin in north-central Maine. Northern Maine has thick forests. In the southeast, lowlands are covered in farmlands and thick pine forests. The Penobscot and Kennebec Rivers run through the center of Maine to the Atlantic Ocean. Bays and **coves** cut into much of Maine's rocky coastline, forming **peninsulas**. In the southwest, sandy beaches cover the coast.

APPALACHIAN MOUNTAINS

10

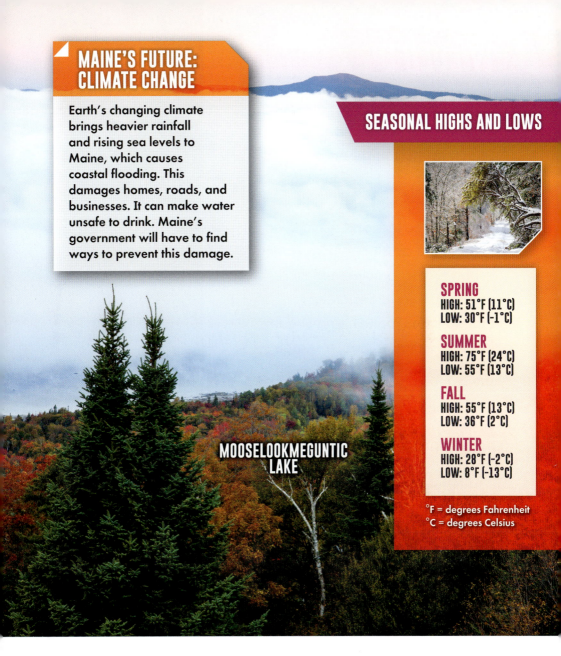

MAINE'S FUTURE: CLIMATE CHANGE

Earth's changing climate brings heavier rainfall and rising sea levels to Maine, which causes coastal flooding. This damages homes, roads, and businesses. It can make water unsafe to drink. Maine's government will have to find ways to prevent this damage.

SEASONAL HIGHS AND LOWS

SPRING
HIGH: 51°F (11°C)
LOW: 30°F (-1°C)

SUMMER
HIGH: 75°F (24°C)
LOW: 55°F (13°C)

FALL
HIGH: 55°F (13°C)
LOW: 36°F (2°C)

WINTER
HIGH: 28°F (-2°C)
LOW: 8°F (-13°C)

°F = degrees Fahrenheit
°C = degrees Celsius

MOOSELOOKMEGUNTIC LAKE

Maine has a **continental** climate. Summers are warm, with cooler temperatures in the north. Winters are cold and snowy. **Nor'easters** bring freezing rain and heavy snowfall. Maine's coast is often foggy throughout the year.

WILDLIFE

Thousands of black bears search for nuts and berries in Maine's forests. Foxes hunt the forests for rabbits, birds, and weasels. Beavers and minks scurry through the brush near riverbanks. Wood turtles, painted turtles, and snapping turtles creep around lakes, ponds, and streams. In the mountains, moose search the slopes for twigs and leaves.

Every spring, Maine's coast and marshes host egrets, herons, and ducks as they travel north. Chickadees, goldfinches, sparrows, and blue jays can be spotted year-round. Water snakes slink through the swamps preying on small fish, frogs, and salamanders.

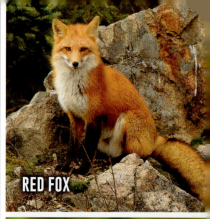
RED FOX

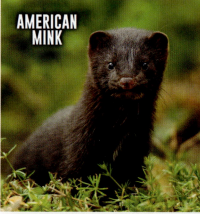
AMERICAN MINK

COMMON SNAPPING TURTLE

COMMON WATER SNAKE

AMERICAN GOLDFINCH

MANY MOOSE
Around 70,000 moose roam Maine's forests and wetlands. Only Alaska has more!

MOOSE
Life Span: up to 22 years
Status: least concern

moose range =

| LEAST CONCERN | NEAR THREATENED | VULNERABLE | ENDANGERED | CRITICALLY ENDANGERED | EXTINCT IN THE WILD | EXTINCT |

PEOPLE AND COMMUNITIES

More than 1.3 million people live in Maine. They are called Mainers. Most Mainers live in **rural** areas. About 4 out of 10 live in cities, such as Maine's largest city of Portland. Lewiston and Bangor are also major cities in Maine.

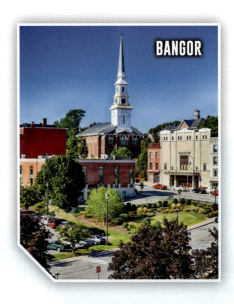
BANGOR

GREENVILLE
RURAL MAINE

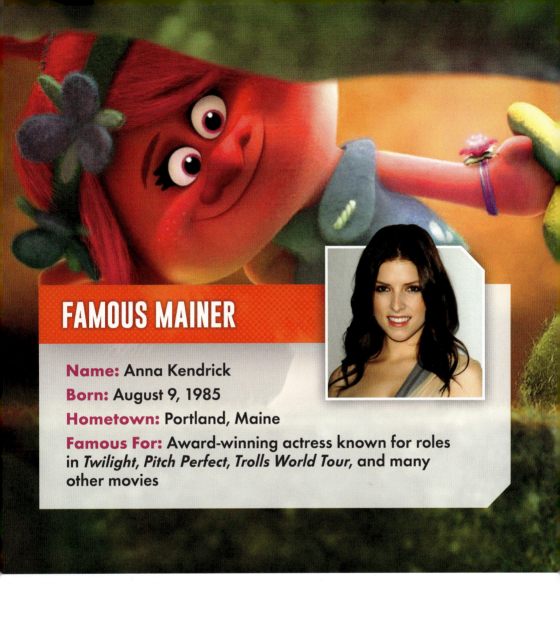

FAMOUS MAINER

Name: Anna Kendrick
Born: August 9, 1985
Hometown: Portland, Maine
Famous For: Award-winning actress known for roles in *Twilight*, *Pitch Perfect*, *Trolls World Tour*, and many other movies

Most Mainers have European **ancestors**. Smaller numbers are Hispanic, African American or Black, or Asian American. There is also a small population of Native Americans in Maine. Some live on **reservations**. Many of Maine's newest **immigrants** come from Canada, the Philippines, Germany, India, and Korea.

PORTLAND

The English first built a settlement around Portland in 1633. It had many names at first. But in 1786, it became known as Portland. Its location on the Atlantic Ocean made Portland an important shipping destination. Fishing was also a key part of its economy.

16

Today, Portland is a major oil port. It sits at the end of the Portland-Montreal oil pipeline. Portland is also a **cultural** center. Visitors browse the city's museums and watch live music or theater performances. Many people enjoy strolling the cobblestone streets of Old Port. Visits to the waterfront on the Eastern Promenade are also popular.

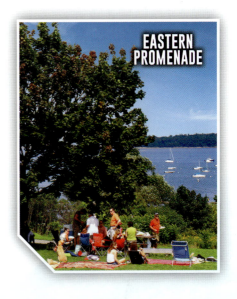

EASTERN PROMENADE

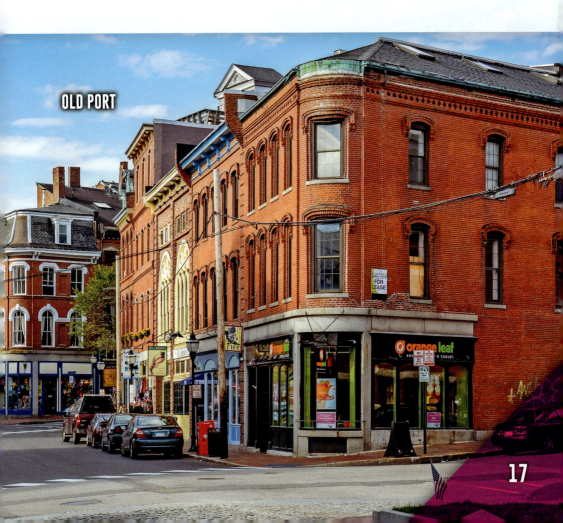

OLD PORT

17

INDUSTRY

During the 1800s, **natural resources** were important to Maine's economy. The state's vast forests led to lumber and shipbuilding businesses. Fishing off its shores also brought in a lot of money. Other big businesses were shoe and fabric **manufacturing**.

MAINE'S FUTURE: NO MORE PAPER

Paper products are important to Maine's economy. But many people now read newspapers, magazines, and books on their computers and phones. Less media needs to be printed. The lower demand for paper might impact Maine's economy.

Today, most Mainers have **service jobs** in hospitals, stores, or restaurants. But natural resources are still important to the economy. Lobster, fish, and other seafood are Maine's largest exports. Mining produces limestone, peat, and copper. Farming is important, too. Farmers grow potatoes, apples, and strawberries. They also collect maple syrup from trees. Maine's top manufactured goods are paper products, wood pulp, and transportation parts.

INVENTED IN MAINE

PRACTICAL DIVE SUIT
Date Invented: 1834
Inventor: Leonard Norcross

EARMUFFS
Date Invented: 1873
Inventor: Chester Greenwood

ZIG-ZAG STITCH
Date Invented: 1873
Inventor: Helen Blanchard

FOOD

LOBSTER ROLL

Maine is known for its seafood. Seasonal lobster shacks serve fresh lobster with butter. Lobster rolls are served on buns with salt, mayo, and lemon. Clam chowder, a creamy soup made with clams, is also popular. Other favorite seafoods include scallops, oysters, and haddock.

CHEERS!
Mainers love Moxie, the official soft drink of Maine. Some say it tastes a little like black licorice. Others compare it to bitter root beer.

20

Other favorite foods are grown in Maine. For a few weeks each spring, fiddleheads are a popular side dish. These coiled ferns only grow in the wild! Wild blueberries are popular in the summertime. They are often mixed into blueberry slump, a sweet dessert made with biscuit dough. Many Mainers also enjoy Maine-style baked beans. Cooks stir maple syrup and salt pork into big pots of beans.

FIDDLEHEADS

CLAM CHOWDER

BLUEBERRY SLUMP

4 SERVINGS

Have an adult help you make this recipe.

INGREDIENTS

2 cups fresh blueberries
1/2 cup sugar
1 cup water
1 cup sifted flour
2 teaspoons baking powder
1/4 teaspoon salt
1/2 cup milk

DIRECTIONS

1. Combine blueberries, sugar, and water in a saucepan. Stew over medium heat.
2. Mix flour, baking powder, and salt in a bowl. Add milk, stirring quickly until dough is slightly moist.
3. When sauce is boiling, drop 2-inch spoonfuls of dough into it. Lower the heat slightly and cover the pan. Cook for about 20 minutes.
4. Spoon dumplings into shallow bowls and cover them with the blueberry sauce. Top with cream or whipped cream if desired.

SPORTS AND ENTERTAINMENT

MAINE RED CLAWS

Many Mainers love sports! College football fans cheer for the University of Maine Black Bears. Baseball fans root for the minor league Portland Sea Dogs. The Maine Red Claws basketball team and the Maine Mariners hockey team also have many fans.

Lakes, beaches, and mountain trails offer endless outdoor adventures. Families explore science and performing arts at the Children's Museum and Theatre of Maine in Portland. Others visit the Maine **Maritime** Museum on the banks of the Kennebec River. Here, they find the only surviving wooden shipyard in the United States!

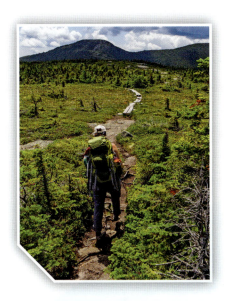

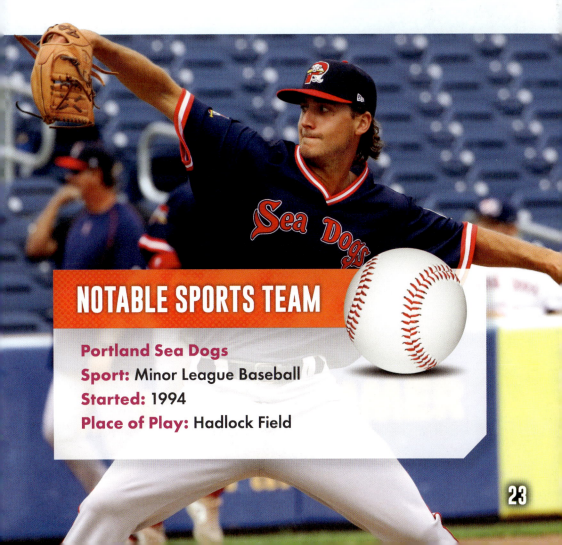

NOTABLE SPORTS TEAM

Portland Sea Dogs
Sport: Minor League Baseball
Started: 1994
Place of Play: Hadlock Field

FESTIVALS AND TRADITIONS

Every August, the Maine Lobster Festival in Rockland features live music, arts and crafts, and a parade. People eat over 20,000 pounds (9,071 kilograms) of lobster during the event! The Machias Wild Blueberry Festival celebrates another famous Maine food. Visitors sample blueberry syrup and enter blueberry pie-eating contests!

U.S. NATIONAL TOBOGGAN CHAMPIONSHIPS
CAMDEN

Long winters do not keep Mainers cooped up. Every winter, people gather in Maine for the U.S. National Toboggan Championships. People race down snow-covered hills on long sleds called toboggans. Sun or snow, Maine is full of fun!

WINDJAMMER DAYS
Windjammer Days is a popular summer festival in Camden, Maine. People gather along the coast to see old-fashioned sailboats called windjammers!

MAINE TIMELINE

1607
English settlers establish the first English colony in Maine

1632
After many years of settlement, the city now known as Portland is named

1818
A treaty establishes Penobscot reservation lands in Maine

1763
The British take full control of Maine from the French

1820
Maine becomes the 23rd state

1919
Lafayette National Park is established, later changed to Acadia National Park in 1929

1832
Maine's capital is moved from Portland to Augusta

1860s
Thousands of Mainers fight in the Union Army during the Civil War

2019
Janet Mills becomes Maine's first female governor

MAINE FACTS

Nickname: The Pine Tree State

Motto: *Dirigo* (I Lead)

Date of Statehood: March 15, 1820 (the 23rd state)

Capital City: Augusta ★

Other Major Cities: Portland, Lewiston, Bangor

Area: 35,380 square miles (91,634 square kilometers); Maine is the 39th largest state.

Population
1,362,359
(2020)

STATE FLAG

The background of Maine's flag is blue. In the middle is the state seal. It shows a moose and a pine tree. These represent the state's natural resources and wildlife. To the left is a farmer, representing agriculture. To the right is a sailor. He represents Maine's ties to the sea. The North Star is at the top of the seal to represent Maine's location. At the bottom of the seal is a light blue banner that says the state's name.

INDUSTRY

JOBS

- MANUFACTURING **7%**
- FARMING AND NATURAL RESOURCES **3%**
- GOVERNMENT **13%**
- SERVICES **77%**

Main Exports

 lobster
 electronics
 fruit
 wood pulp and paper
 transportation equipment

Natural Resources
lumber, seafood, sand, gravel, limestone, slate, crushed stone

GOVERNMENT

4 ELECTORAL VOTES

Federal Government
2 REPRESENTATIVES | **2** SENATORS

 ME

USA

State Government
151 REPRESENTATIVES | **35** SENATORS

STATE SYMBOLS

STATE BIRD
BLACK-CAPPED CHICKADEE

STATE ANIMAL
MOOSE

STATE FLOWER
WHITE PINE CONE AND TASSEL

STATE TREE
WHITE PINE

GLOSSARY

ancestors—relatives who lived long ago

colony—a distant territory which is under the control of another nation

continental—referring to a climate that has hot summers and cold winters, such as those found in central North America and Asia

coves—small, sheltered bays

cultural—relating to the beliefs, arts, and ways of life in a place or society

immigrants—people who move to a new country

manufacturing—a field of work in which people use machines to make products

maritime—relating to navigation or trade on the sea

natural resources—materials in the earth that are taken out and used to make products or fuel

New England—an area in the northeastern United States that includes Maine, New Hampshire, Vermont, Massachusetts, Rhode Island, and Connecticut

nor'easters—large storms that hit coastal northeastern states; winds blow in from the northeast.

peninsulas—sections of land that extend out from larger pieces of land and are almost completely surrounded by water

reservations—areas of land that are controlled by Native American tribes

Revolutionary War—the war from 1775 to 1783 in which the United States fought for independence from Great Britain

rural—related to the countryside

service jobs—jobs that perform tasks for people or businesses

settlers—people who move to live in a new, undeveloped region

TO LEARN MORE

AT THE LIBRARY

Doak, Robin S. *Maine*. New York, N.Y.: Children's Press, 2018.

Nelson, Penelope S. *Acadia National Park*. Minneapolis, Minn.: Jump!, 2020.

Ogintz, Eileen. *The Kid's Guide to Maine*. Camden, Maine: Down East Books, 2018.

ON THE WEB

Factsurfer.com gives you a safe, fun way to find more information.

1. Go to www.factsurfer.com.

2. Enter "Maine" into the search box and click 🔍.

3. Select your book cover to see a list of related content.

INDEX

arts, 17, 23
Atlantic Ocean, 5, 6, 7, 10, 16
Augusta, 6, 7
Bangor, 7, 14
Cadillac Mountain, 4–5
capital (see Augusta)
climate, 11, 25
fast facts, 28–29
festivals, 24–25
food, 20–21, 24
future, 11, 18
history, 8–9, 16, 18
inventions, 19
Kendrick, Anna, 15
Kennebec River, 6, 7, 10, 23
landmarks, 5, 17, 23
landscape, 10–11, 12, 23
Lewiston, 7, 14
location, 6–7
Machias Wild Blueberry
   Festival, 24
Maine Lobster Festival, 24

Mount Desert Island, 6, 7
outdoor activities, 17, 23, 25
people, 8, 9, 14–15
Portland, 7, 14, 15, 16–17, 23
Portland Sea Dogs, 22, 23
recipe, 21
Revolutionary War, 8, 9
size, 6
sports, 22, 23, 25
timeline, 26–27
U.S. National Toboggan
   Championships, 25
wildlife, 12–13
Windjammer Days, 25
working, 16, 18–19

The images in this book are reproduced through the courtesy of: Sean Pavone, front cover, pp. 2–3, 5 (Old Fort Western), 16; Yellowj , p. 3 (lobster); Doug Lemke, pp. 4–5; Wade H. Massie, p. 5 (Gulf Hagas); Enrico Della Pietra, p. 5 (Nubble Lighthouse); Wangkun Jia, p. 5 (Portland Observatory); North Wind Picture Archives/ Alamy, p. 8; Jon Arnold Images Ltd/ Alamy, p. 9; Jonathan A. Mauer, pp. 10, 23 (hiking); Stacy Funderburke, p. 11 (Mooselookmeguntic Lake); Ann Stryzhekin, p. 11 (inset); Michiel de Wit, p. 12 (common water snake); Rejean Bedard, p. 12 (red fox); An inspiration, p. 12 (American mink); Tyler Clemons, p. 12 (common snapping turtle); Matt Inman, p. 12 (American goldfinch); Richard Seeley, p. 13; traveler1116, p. 14 (Bangor); DenisTangneyJr, p. 14 (Greenville); AF archive/ Alamy, p. 15 (Trolls World Tour); Everett Collection, p. 15 (Anna Kendrick); Jeffrey Isaac Greenberg 3+/ Alamy, p. 17 (Eastern Promenade); jejim, p. 17 (Old Port); Stuart Monk, p. 18; Oleksiy Mark, p. 18 (No More Paper); Kevin Shields/ Alamy, p. 19; toozdesign, p. 19 (practical dive suit); Petr Malyshev, p. 19 (earmuffs); Lasmane, p. 19 (zig-zag stitch); Brent Hofacker, pp. 20 (lobster roll), 21 (fiddleheads); Wikipedia, pp. 20 (Moxie), 21 (blueberry slump), 26 (1820), 27 (Janet Mills); karins, p. 21 (clam chowder); Bukhta Yurii, p. 21 (blueberries); ZUMA Press, Inc./ Alamy, pp. 22, 23 (Portland Sea Dogs); Wangkun Jia, p. 24; Portland Press Herald/ Getty Images, p. 25 (U.S. National Toboggan Championships); Jeff Schultes, p. 25 (Windjammer Days); Jon Bilous, pp. 26–27, 28–29, 30–31, 32; Eric Urquhart, p. 27 (Acadia National Park); Millenius, p. 28 (flag); Michael G. Mill, p. 29 (black-capped chickadee); Michael Liggett, p. 29 (moose); Avalon.red/ Alamy, p. 29 (white pine cone and tassel); Gerald D. Tang, p. 29 (white pine); Tsekhmister, p. 31 (honeybee).